汉语桥－中学生夏令营
Chinese Bridge Summer Camp for Foreign Students

中国欢迎你
Welcome to China　短期汉语系列教材

Xue Lianpu

学脸谱
Lianpu

才艺类

高等教育出版社·北京
HIGHER EDUCATION PRESS　BEIJING

"中国欢迎你"短期汉语系列教材

总策划　许　琳

总监制　王永利

策　划　陈　默　　邵亦鹏

监　制　薛　佼

编委会成员（按姓名音序排列）

常　春	迟兰英	代凝慧	丁　磊	丁　颖	董　赟
范祖奎	冯丽君	郝永宁	贺红梅	侯晓彬	纪仁盛
贾静芳	贾腾飞	姜志琪	金飞飞	鞠　慧	孔庆国
孔雪晴	李红艳	李　娜	梁小岸	梁　云	刘芳珍
刘玉波	卢小燕	罗来莉	罗兴平	孟宪滨	秦晓燕
屠晓蓓	汪正才	王　岱	王文龙	王　艳	王　瑜
王玉静	温　培	吴玉为	席忠祥	许　娟	杨　硕
杨晓霞	袁　勇	张　蕾	张　丽	张全生	张新江
张　勇	章新拓	赵江民	郑　颖	周　芳	周　荧
朱　璇	朱　芸				

前言

随着中国与世界各国距离的拉近，越来越多的人渴望了解中国、体验中国。为了帮助"汉语桥"夏令营中小学生以及所有对中国感兴趣的外国朋友在较短时间内了解中国的语言和文化、历史与风俗，中国国家汉办/孔子学院总部组织研发了"中国欢迎你"短期汉语系列教材。

◉ 适用对象 ▶

本系列教材主要适用于来华参加夏令营的海外中小学生，也可用于海外孔子学院和孔子课堂作为汉语教学辅助资源。

◉ 教材构成 ▶

本系列教材分为三大类：语言类、才艺类和地域类。

《学脸谱》是才艺类教材中的一册，主要内容包括中国脸谱介绍、脸谱绘画与制作、脸谱图案等。本书将文化与才艺学习有机地结合起来，同时配以丰富的练习和活动，目的在于帮助学习者在较短时间内了解中国脸谱的基本知识，掌握脸谱的基本绘画技能。本书的参考教学时间为6～8学时。

◉ 编写特色 ▶

1. 全新的编写理念：本系列教材借鉴了全新的外语教学理念和最先进的外语教学法成果，真正做到以学习者为中心，满足学习者的个性化需求。

2. 全新的编写风格：本系列教材话题实用，内容简单，形式丰富，图文并茂，寓教于乐，注重实效，目的在于使汉语变得"易懂、易学、易用"。

3. 全新的教学设计：本系列教材以任务和活动为主线，便于教师进行教学设计，充分调动学习者的兴趣，实现轻松有效的课堂教学。

让我们翻开书，一起去感知充满魅力的汉语和中国文化！

编委会

2011年5月

Contents 目录

Lianpu

脸 谱

Introduction to Lianpu 脸谱介绍

"Lianpu" is the Chinese operatic art of painting the faces of the actors. Theatrical make-up is a fine art used in performance mainly to enhance the role of character in the story and to express their characteristics. There are many styles of lianpu. For example, Beijing opera, with its attention to the use of color and rich patterns, is considered to represent traditional Chinese culture. Beijing opera is enjoyed by audiences both at home and abroad.

Lianpu is visually beautiful; the actors' faces are vividly colored and wonderfully exaggerated. The artistry of lianpu can be enjoyed on stage and each mask can also be appreciated individually.

脸谱是中国戏曲演员脸上的绘画，是舞台演出时的化妆造型艺术，主要用于表现角色的性格特征等。在众多的脸谱门类中，京剧脸谱以其用色讲究、图案丰富、体系完整而被认为是中华民族传统文化的标识，深受海内外朋友的喜爱。

脸谱美在直观，美在夸张，美在色彩。它既可以在舞台上欣赏，又可以拿出来单独欣赏。

Lianpu originates from the stage, but we can also see evidence of it in real life: in different styles of architecture, in colorful product-packaging, and in the design of daily-use items and clothing. The artistic creativity behind lianpu is readily seen. Now, let's head into the mysterious and fascinating world of Chinese lianpu.

脸谱来源于舞台，但在现实生活中，我们不难在建筑物、商品包装、日常用品或服饰上看到风格迥异的脸谱形象，脸谱强大的艺术生命力可见一斑。现在，让我们一起走进神奇而迷人的脸谱世界吧。

🔍 True or False? 判断正误

1. Lianpu is used in operatic performances mainly to show the character's age.
   脸谱主要用于表现舞台角色的年龄。 　　　　　　　　　(　)

2. Beijing opera is an important representative of Chinese opera lianpu techniques.
   京剧脸谱是众多戏曲脸谱的一个突出的代表。 　　　　　(　)

3. Lianpu is an art used on stage which originates from daily life for "masking" ordinary products.
   舞台上的脸谱化妆来源于生活中的工艺美术脸谱制品。 　(　)

📖 Knowledge Links 知识链接

Styles of Lianpu in Beijing Opera 京剧脸谱的样式

整脸
Zhenglian (single-color style)

三块瓦脸
Sankuaiwalian (tri-color style)

十字门脸
Shizimenlian (cross-pattern style)

碎花脸
Suihualian (complex style)

歪脸
Wailian (imbalanced style)

Lianpu and the Characters in Beijing Opera
京剧脸谱与角色

In Beijing opera, the four main character roles are: "*sheng*," "*dan*," "*jing*," and "*chou*." *Sheng* and *dan* roles use relatively simple facial make-up. Face-painting is primarily for the *jing* and *chou* characters.

- *Sheng* are the leading male roles.
- *Dan* are the female roles.
- *Jing* are the roles that have vivid characteristics and exaggerated painting.
- *Chou* are funny, clownish roles.

　　在京剧中，主要有生、旦、净、丑四大行当。"生"和"旦"两个行当面部化妆简单，略施脂粉，所以脸谱化妆主要用于"净"和"丑"两个行当。

- "生"主要是男性角色。
- "旦"主要是女性角色。
- "净"是画有夸张脸谱的性格鲜明的角色。
- "丑"是滑稽、可笑的小丑角色。

生（诸葛亮）
Sheng Zhuge Liang

旦（杨玉环）
Dan Yang Yuhuan

净（曹操）
Jing Cao Cao

丑（蒋干）
Chou Jiang Gan

项羽

Xiang Yu, the Conqueror

💡 Let's Think 想一想

According to the lianpu on the left, guess what kind of character role he plays.

通过脸谱判断，图中的人物应该属于哪个行当？

🔥 Knowledge Links 知识链接

Zhuge Liang: He was an outstanding politician, strategist and inventor during the Three Kingdoms Period. According to historical records, Zhuge Liang was enormously intelligent and good at predictions. Besides his achievements in the fields of military affairs and politics, he was also very accomplished in painting, music and literature.

诸葛亮：三国时期杰出的政治家、军事家、发明家。历史上记载的诸葛亮聪明过人，料事如神，除了在军事和政治方面很有成就之外，他在书画、音乐和文学方面也都颇有才能。

Yang Yuhuan: Also known as the Royal Concubine Yang, Yang Yuhuan was the favorite concubine of Emperor Xuanzong of the Tang Dynasty. She is renowned as one of the four great beauties in ancient China. Emperor Xuanzong was very fond of her; she was talented in singing and dancing. The emperor indulged himself in comforts with her and ignored state affairs. During an armed rebellion, due to demands from the army, Royal Concubine Yang was forced to hang herself.

杨玉环：也叫杨贵妃，唐玄宗的宠妃，中国古代四大美女之一。唐玄宗非常喜爱擅长歌舞、精通音律的杨贵妃，每日沉迷于酒色歌舞之中，不理政事。在一次叛乱中，在众多将士的压力下，杨贵妃被逼自尽。

Cao Cao: As a strategist, politician and poet, Cao Cao laid the foundation to establish the Wei Kingdom during the Three Kingdoms Period. He knew military tactics very well and spent his entire life in battle. In spite of his talents and achievements, Cao Cao was depicted as a deceitful, envious and cunning man, enthusiastic for power in Beijing Opera performances.

曹操：军事家、政治家和诗人，三国时期魏国的主要缔造者。他一生征战，精于兵法，是个很有才能的人。不过在京剧表演中，曹操被认为是一个性格奸诈、爱猜忌、善用狡诈手段谋取大权的野心家。

Jiang Gan: He was subordinate to Cao Cao during the Three Kingdoms Period and was a famous orator. In the masterpiece "*Romance of the Three Kingdoms*," Jiang was portrayed as a pitiful man. During the classic "War of *Chibi*," Jiang fell into a trap set by his enemies and stole a fake letter, which resulted in Cao Cao's wrongful killing of two important generals.

蒋干：三国时期曹操的幕僚，善于辩论。在《三国演义》中，他被刻画成小丑的形象。在赤壁之战的时候，他中计偷了一封假书信，导致曹操错杀了两员大将。

Lianpu and Color in Beijing Opera
京剧脸谱与颜色

Color is the language of lianpu. Colors are not randomly drawn and each color has its own meaning. Each Beijing opera mask has its own main color and also other colors which accent the main color. Different colors represent the personalities of the different characters.

　　色彩是脸谱的语言，每种颜色都代表不同的含义，尤其是京剧脸谱，色彩讲究，每个脸谱都有一个主色，辅以其他的配色，不同的色彩代表了不同的人物性格。

🔋 Chinese Learning 汉语加油站

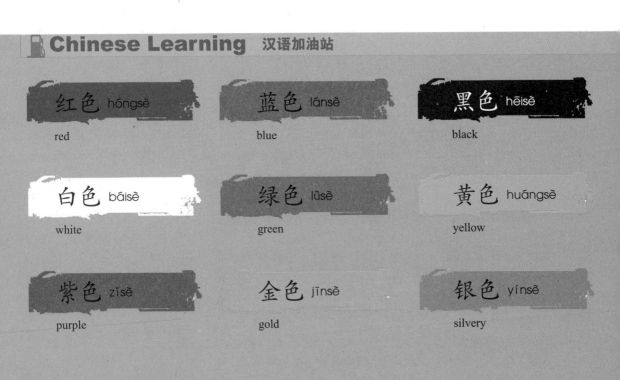

红色 hóngsè	蓝色 lánsè	黑色 hēisè
red	blue	black
白色 báisè	绿色 lǜsè	黄色 huángsè
white	green	yellow
紫色 zǐsè	金色 jīnsè	银色 yínsè
purple	gold	silvery

● 红色(hóngsè)：忠诚、勇敢
Red: loyal, brave

● 蓝色(lánsè)：刚强、有心计
Blue: unyielding, calculating

● 黑色(hēisè)：正直、刚直、智慧
Black: upright and outspoken, intelligent

● 紫色(zǐsè)：刚正、沉着、不媚权贵
Purple: upright, calm, not sucking up to influential figures

○ 白色(báisè)：奸诈、多疑
White: treacherous, overly suspicious

● 绿色(lǜsè)：勇猛、莽撞
Green: bold and powerful, reckless

● 黄色(huángsè)：勇猛、暴躁
Yellow: bold and powerful, hot-tempered

● 金色(jīnsè)和银色(yínsè)：神仙、高人
Gold and Silvery: an immortal or a highly-skilled person

1. Look at the pictures and count the number of each kind of lianpu.

    看图片，数出各种脸谱的数量。

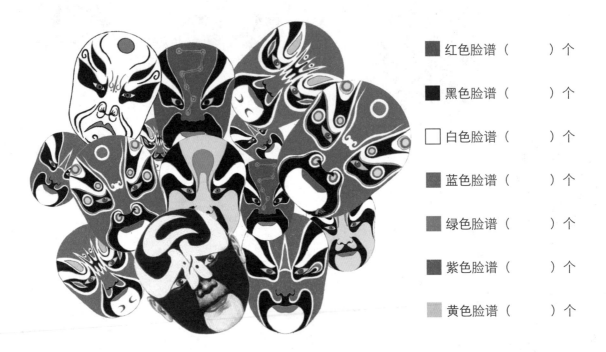

■ 红色脸谱（　　）个

■ 黑色脸谱（　　）个

□ 白色脸谱（　　）个

■ 蓝色脸谱（　　）个

■ 绿色脸谱（　　）个

■ 紫色脸谱（　　）个

■ 黄色脸谱（　　）个

2. If the following characters were roles in a Beijing opera, what color of lianpu would they wear?

    如果京剧中有下面的人物角色，应该用什么颜色的脸谱？

超人
Superman

宙斯
Zeus

《白雪公主》中的皇后
the Queen in "*Snow White*"

Lianpu Patterns of Beijing Opera 京剧脸谱与图案

There are many lianpu patterns, rich in design and varying with each role. There are no specific rules for the patterns.

脸谱图案非常丰富，每个部位的图案变化多端，有规律而无定律。

✂ Match 连一连

Look at the patterns of the masks below, what does each represent?
连连看，下面的脸谱图案分别表示什么意思？

龙形眉毛
Dragon-shaped
eyebrows

葫芦图案
Gourd pattern

阴阳图
Yinyang pattern

月牙图案
Crescent-shaped
pattern

兵器图案
Weapons pattern

皇帝
Emperor

清正廉洁
Upright and honest

喜欢喝酒
Likes to drink wine

神机妙算
Man of foresight

善武
Good at kung fu

Putting on Beijing Opera Make-up
京剧脸谱化妆

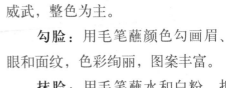

Beijing opera actors need to use a special face-paint, however, there are several different ways to put the make-up on.

Rubbing: Use your fingers to rub the base color all over the face, and then add the colors of the pattern to make the imposing impression of a full-color mask.

Drawing: Use a brush dipped in bright colors to outline the eyebrows, the eyes and other rich patterns.

Wiping: Use a brush dipped in water and white powder to smear the whole face (or part of the face) with white; this will draw attention to a treacherous villain.

京剧脸谱化妆需要用专门的油彩，主要有以下三种化妆方式：

揉脸：用手指将颜色揉满面部，再加重面部纹理的描画，凝重威武，整色为主。

勾脸：用毛笔蘸颜色勾画眉、眼和面纹，色彩绚丽，图案丰富。

抹脸：用毛笔蘸水和白粉，把全脸或一部分涂抹成白色，突出坏人的奸诈。

💡 Let's Think 想一想

1. What method does an actor usually use to put on white make-up?
   白色脸谱通常使用以上哪种化妆方式？

2. Is face-painting put on starting from the middle towards the two sides of the face or from the two sides of the face towards the middle?
   脸谱化妆是从中间向两边画还是从两边向中间画？

Drawing and Hand-making
脸谱绘画与制作

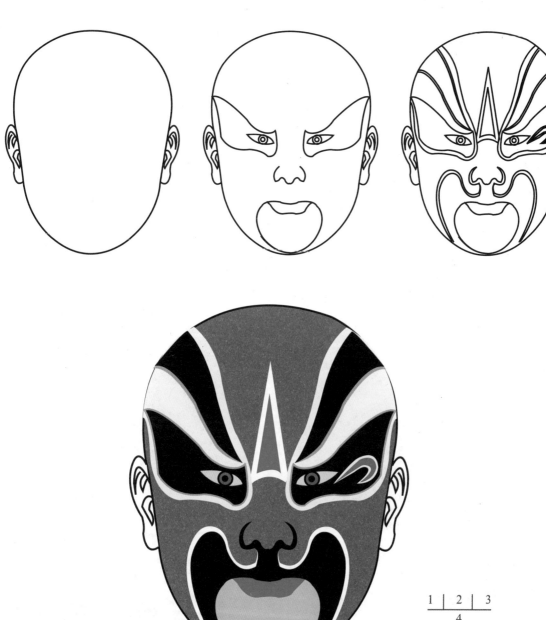

⟨⟩ **Try It Yourself** 试一试

Using the picture on page 11 as a guide, draw a painted-face. Compare everyone's picture and see whose picture is most like the original.

仿照第11页的图片画一张脸谱图。比一比谁画的图片最接近原图。

     Drawing and Hand-making │ 脸谱绘画与制作

1. Follow the teacher and learn to sing a song about lianpu. 在老师的带领下，学唱一段关于脸谱的中国歌曲。

♩ = 150

蓝脸的窦尔敦　　　盗　御马，　　　红脸的关　公　　　战长沙，
lán liǎn de dòu ěr dūn　　dào　yù mǎ　　　hóng liǎn de guān gōng　　zhǎn cháng shā

黄脸的典韦，　　白脸的曹操，　　黑脸的张　飞　叫
huáng liǎn de diǎn wěi　　bāi liǎn de cáo cāo　　hēi liǎn de zhāng　　fēi　jiào

喳　喳。
zhā　zhā

Lyrics 歌词

Blue-faced Dou Erdun steals a royal horse,　　蓝脸的窦尔敦盗御马，

Red-faced Guan Gong battles in Changsha,　　红脸的关公战长沙，

Yellow-faced Dian Wei,　　黄脸的典韦，

White-faced Cao Cao,　　白脸的曹操，

Black-faced Zhang Fei is making a loud noise.　　黑脸的张飞叫喳喳。

2. According to the patterns on pages 17 and 18, draw lianpu for the characters in the song on five pieces of paper. Hold up the corresponding masks according to what your teacher sings.

根据第17~18页提供的图样，在五张纸上分别画出歌曲中的人物脸谱。将画好的五张脸谱放在桌子上，根据老师唱的内容，举起相应的脸谱图片。

3. Make groups of five to act out the song about lianpu. See which group does the best job.

五个学生一组，利用脸谱图片共同表演歌曲《说唱脸谱》。比比哪组表演得最好。

Make a Lianpu Bookmark 做脸谱书签

Choose a lianpu pattern from pages 19 and 20 and make a lianpu bookmark.
在19～20页的脸谱图案中选一个你喜欢的图案，按照下面的步骤做一个脸谱书签吧。

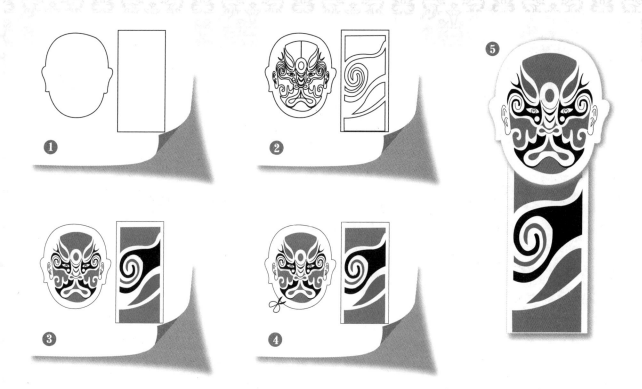

① Draw the outline of the bookmark on cardboard. 在硬纸板上画出书签轮廓。

② Paint the lianpu. 画脸谱。

③ Color the lianpu. 涂色。

④ Cut out the bookmark and stick it well. 剪下书签，并粘合好。

⑤ Finished. 完成。

A Lianpu Art Show
脸谱制作秀

Lianpu can be painted on fans, playing cards, T-shirts, and other products. Use your imagination, pick your favorite handicraft or household item, and draw a lianpu on it. Then, with your classmates, display these items in a lianpu art show.

脸谱的装饰性很强，比如可以画在扇面、扑克牌、T恤衫等物品上。请发挥你的想象，挑选一个你喜欢的工艺品或生活用品，把脸谱画在上面。做好后和同学们一起举办一个小型的脸谱作品展吧。

Lianpu Patterns 脸谱图案

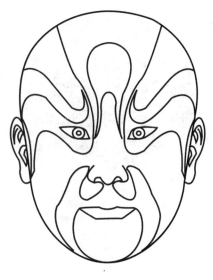

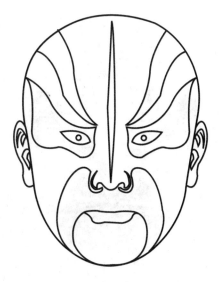

Answers 答案

 True or False? 判断正误

1. (F)   2. (T)   3. (F)

 Let's Think 想一想

The lianpu of the figure on the picture is made by colorful oil paint and the patterns are complicated. This is *jing* in Beijing opera.

图中的人物脸谱以重色油彩勾画，图案复杂，属于京剧中的净行。

Let's Think 想一想

1. 红色脸谱（2）个   黑色脸谱（1）个   白色脸谱（1）个   蓝色脸谱（3）个
   绿色脸谱（3）个   紫色脸谱（2）个   黄色脸谱（2）个

2. (For reference) Superman uses the red lianpu, which stands for loyalty and bravery. Zeus uses the gold or silvery lianpu, which is for gods or goddesses. The queen in "*Snow White*" uses the white lianpu, which represents a false or fraudulent character.

   （本答案仅供参考）超人用红色脸谱，代表忠诚和勇敢；宙斯是神，用金色或银色脸谱；《白雪公主》中的皇后用白色脸谱，表现性格的奸诈。

Match 连一连

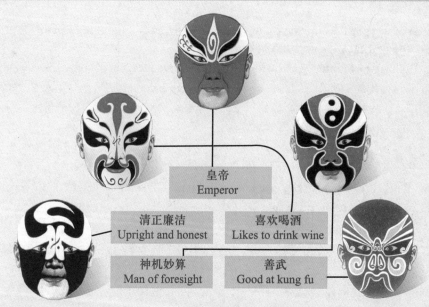

皇帝
Emperor

清正廉洁
Upright and honest

喜欢喝酒
Likes to drink wine

神机妙算
Man of foresight

善武
Good at kung fu

◆ **The crescent on Baogong's forehead indicates his integrity. 包公的月牙图案表示清正廉洁。**
It was said that Baogong got injured in his youth and had a scar on his forehead. To create his image of honesty and integrity on the stage, people added the pattern of a white crescent on Baogong's forehead. The crescent implies perceptiveness and it carries a mysterious atmosphere.

It signifies that Baogong can judge the earthly lawsuits during daytime and judge unfair matters in the underground world during nighttime.

传说包公年少时不小心受伤，额头上留下了一道浅疤。戏曲舞台为了塑造清官形象，在包公额头上添画了一道白色月牙，月牙寓意明察一切，又带有一点神秘的色彩，表现包公可以"日断阳，夜断阴"，即白天能审人世间的冤案，夜里断判地狱中的不平。

◆ **Meng Liang's bottle gourd pattern shows his addiction to alcohol. 孟良的葫芦图案表示他喜欢喝酒。** Since the bottle gourd is light weight and easy to carry, and liquor stored in a bottle gourd is unlikely to deteriorate, during ancient times bottle gourds were often used as containers for liquor before plastics and glass were invented. The pattern of the red bottle gourd on Meng Liang's forehead is a sign that Meng Liang is fond of drinking alcohol.

由于葫芦重量轻，便于携带，酒存放在葫芦中又不易变质，在没有塑料和玻璃的古代，葫芦常常作为装酒的容器。孟良额头上有一个红色的葫芦，用来表示他喜欢喝酒。

◆ **The dragon-shaped eyebrow shows that Zhao Kuangyin is an emperor. 赵匡胤的龙眉表示他是皇帝。** The dragon is the symbol for the emperor in ancient China. Drawing a dragon-shaped eyebrow for the role Zhao Kuangyin is to highlight his position of emperor.

龙在中国古代是帝王的象征，所以赵匡胤画龙眉是为了表示他是皇帝。

◆ **The *yinyang* on Jiang Wei's forehead is a sign of his clever strategies and shrewd tactics. 姜维额头画有阴阳图表示神机妙算。** The *yinyang* is used for observing space in ancient China. The *yinyang* on Jiang Wei's forehead is a symbol of his clever strategies and his ability to predict the future.

阴阳图，是中国古代表示宇宙观像的图，姜维头上的阴阳图表示他神机妙算，有预见未来的能力。

◆ **The pattern of weapons on the lianpu of Dou Erdun expresses his courage and skillful actions in battle. 窦尔墩的脸谱的兵器图案表示他英勇善武。** Lianpu in Beijing Opera often presents a character's iconic weapon. The pattern of double hooks on the lianpu of Dou Erdun indicates his courage and bravery in battle.

京剧脸谱中经常画有人物擅长使用的兵器。窦尔敦的脸谱中画一对双钩以表示其英勇善武。

 Let's Think 想一想　　　　　　　　　　　　　　　　　　**第10页**

1. White lianpu is used for cunning and suspicious characters. The main method is to wipe the whole face, that is, to dip the brush in water and white power and make the whole face, or part of the face, white.

白色脸谱主要用于表现性格奸诈、多疑的人，主要的化妆方式是抹脸，即用毛笔蘸水和白粉，把全脸或一部分涂抹成白色。

2. While drawing the lianpu, one needs to apply white paint onto all parts except for the forehead, eyebrow, nose and mouth. After finishing painting the outline, the patterns on the features are painted. One goes from the two sides to the middle when painting the lianpu.

画脸谱要先用白色勾画脑门、眉、鼻、嘴以外的部位，画完外部大致轮廓后，再用油彩勾画中间图案。所以，画脸谱是从两边向中间画。

郑重声明

高等教育出版社依法对本书享有专有出版权。任何未经许可的复制、销售行为均违反《中华人民共和国著作权法》，其行为人将承担相应的民事责任和行政责任；构成犯罪的，将被依法追究刑事责任。为了维护市场秩序，保护读者的合法权益，避免读者误用盗版书造成不良后果，我社将配合行政执法部门和司法机关对违法犯罪的单位和个人进行严厉打击。社会各界人士如发现上述侵权行为，希望及时举报，本社将奖励举报有功人员。

反盗版举报电话　　（010）58581897 58582371 58581879
反盗版举报传真　　（010）82086060
反盗版举报邮箱　　dd@hep.com.cn
通信地址　　北京市西城区德外大街4号　高等教育出版社法务部
邮政编码　　100120

图书在版编目（CIP）数据

学脸谱 / 国家汉办 / 孔子学院总部编著 . 一北京：高等教育出版
社，2011.6（2013.6 重印）

《中国欢迎你》短期汉语系列教材

ISBN 978-7-04-032034-3

Ⅰ . ①学… Ⅱ . ①国… Ⅲ . ①汉语—阅读教学—对外汉语教学
—教学参考资料 Ⅳ . ① H195.4

中国版本图书馆 CIP 数据核字（2011）第 101721 号

策划编辑	周　芳	责任编辑	鞠　慧	封面设计	乔　剑	版式设计	悦尔视觉
责任绘图	悦尔视觉	插图选配	鞠　慧	责任校对	鞠　慧　刘映荻	责任印制	朱学忠

出版发行	高等教育出版社	咨询电话	400-810-0598
社　　址	北京市西城区德外大街4号	网　　址	http://www.hep.edu.cn
邮政编码	100120		http://www.hep.com.cn
印　　刷	北京信彩瑞禾印刷厂	网上订购	http://www.landraco.com
开　　本	787×1092　1/16		http://www.landraco.com.cn
印　　张	1.75	版　　次	2011 年 6 月第 1 版
字　　数	44 000	印　　次	2013 年 6 月第 3 次印刷
购书热线	010-58581118	定　　价	13.80元

本书如有缺页、倒页、脱页等质量问题，请到所购图书销售部门联系调换

版权所有　侵权必究

物 料 号　32034-00